Caresses and Wounds

Poems by Bob Savino

Kansas City   Spartan Press   Missouri

Spartan Press
Kansas City, Missouri
spartanpresskc.com

Copyright (c) Bob Savino, 2018
First Edition 1 3 5 7 9 10 8 6 4 2
ISBN: 978-1-946642-48-6
LCCN: 2018937040

Design, edits and layout: Jason Ryberg
Cover art: Bob Savino
Author photo: Charles Stonewall
All rights reserved. No part of this publication may be reproduced or transmitted in any form or by any means, electronic or mechanical, including photocopying, recording or by info retrieval system, without prior written permission from the author.

Spartan Press would like to thank Prospero's Books, The Fellowship of N-finite Jest, The Prospero Institute of Disquieted P/o/e/t/i/c/s, Will Leathem, Tom Wayne, Jeanette Powers, j.d.tulloch, Jon Bidwell, Jason Preu, Mark McClane, Tony Hayden and the whole Osage Arts Community.

CONTENTS

Hideout / 1

Still On The Run / 2

Tough Love / 3

The City At Dusk / 4

Carpe Diem / 5

Climate Change / 6

Night Comes On / 7

At The Brink / 8

The Mists / 9

Realities / 10

A Small White Dog / 11

Cracked Open / 13

The Balm / 14

The Knot / 15

Spellbinder / 16

I Heard You Say It / 17

Blood Moon Prayer / 18

Turning Point / 20

Invitation / 21

Quandary / 22

Sleepless After A Fight / 23

Slaphappy Psalm / 24

Crash Landing / 25

Here On Earth / 26

The Splendor / 28

Hearing Wind Gust / 29

Darker Crimson / 30

The Wound / 31

Birth Throes / 32

Riddle / 33

Shouting Hello / 34

Over The Moon / 35

The Arrow / 36

Somebody Named Me / 37

Soul's Needle / 38

Caresses And Wounds / 39

After The Election / 40

Family Reunion / 42

A Handful Of Confetti / 43

Detachment / 45

As Above So Below / 47

Grains Of Silence / 48

Desert Nights / 49

Divine Stalking / 50

North Wind / 51

Messenger / 52

Excerpts From the Demon Tactics Guide / 53

The Limits / 54

Invoking The Muse / 55

Shining Ones / 56

Metamorphosis / 57

Do I contradict myself?
Very well, I contradict myself.
I am large, I contain multitudes.

-Walt Whitman

HIDEOUT

clinging to the underside of a leaf fragile wings
folded   as raindrops strike its surface my soul
lies low in the magical darkness   far removed
from timetables deadlines checklists agendas

if there's some secret passage to another world
it's this   where time dissolves into timelessness
here every splash of rain is rare strange new
listen   our sentient planet's murmuring to itself

have you a safe refuge for the absconding soul
a holy place beyond the clutch of life or death?
without one we drown in obsession and illusion
go now   take flight   your hideout's in Eternity!

STILL ON THE RUN

fear   that squirmy biter in the dark   chasing me
all my life I've been running   while at my heels--
snapping jaws! hard to run anymore   just limping
trying to stay ahead of death's latest zombie clone

cotton mouth   scatterbrain panic   fate's plaything
the bogyman's gonna get me! no safe place to hide!
I zig   then zag   but so does my demon   stalking me
I turn at bay   shake my fists   hell laughs in my face

don't want to give up   yet I'm wearing down   soon
I'll stop in my tracks   fling wide my arms   howling
Come get me motherfucker! oh--how it will feed!
I'll taste the depths of my terror   then I'll be free

TOUGH LOVE

intimate   elemental   a cold wind
stalks outside   agitating branches
just beyond my flimsy windowpane

winter's coming it warns   and one
will break you   will be your last

of those close companions I trust
it's the wind that pulls no punches
unsentimental   straight to the bone

tough love   taking my breath away!
but hugs and kisses don't always work

strange   to feel comforted by chaos--
the sky's slap! emptiness with attitude!
a rough bodyguard named The Universe

some night I'll plunge into its gusty void
and keep going--star after star after star...

THE CITY AT DUSK

visible from space   the city at dusk
scintillates   a capsized constellation

or it may be the galactic mother ship
arrived in splendor to gather us home

drugs   knifings   drive-by shootings
still plague   devour   but camouflaged

with enough distance even the worst
goes veiled in the bedazzle of miracle!

stark silhouettes braille against a sky
set aflame by sunset's guttering glow

bare trees   the crisscrossed branches
they stitch together twin firmaments

glyphs that spell *as above so below*
arteries binding the city to the stars

CARPE DIEM

juicy blackberries and banana slices over granola
soaking in a bath of milk and cream   along with
half an *everything* bagel   a glass of apple cider

morning slants in stripes through the mini-blinds
capping a good night's sleep and a luminous dream
about a sacred child and a father with cobalt eyes

an old man can feel like a flea under death's armpit
yet alive and still kicking on this sun-drenched day
what else can I do but slingshot my voice in praise!

outside my window a cold wind racks the branches
inside raggedy slippers all ten toes curl and uncurl
heartbeat by heartbeat I kiss each second as it flies!

CLIMATE CHANGE

this morning   I can't stop obsessing about
torture   the latest poll shows almost 50%
of Americans approve   OK let's start with
your mother--waterboard'er till she breaks!

we're going insane   has anybody noticed?
we're hooked by the latest commercial jingle
but no longer hear the Music of the Spheres
I wonder who today's mass murderer will be?

it's always about the soul   but since the soul
can't be quantified and morphed into money
we shunt it aside   maybe it's up in the attic
or down in the basement under a pile of rags

when we meet   you stare straight through me
flashing a dead smile   this is not a good sign!
when you laugh   my chilled bones shudder
I begin to question how things will turn out

we need some way to get back to square one
to that child inside   buried alive   screaming
otherwise   hate's hurricanes will metastasize
the oceans will keep on rising until we drown

NIGHT COMES ON

one bright star glitters low in the west
   caught at the fringe of a long dark cloud
      the sky deepens from blue to indigo

two dark clouds sprawl low in the west
   a vee of geese wings toward the horizon
      the sky deepens as night comes on

the sky deepens   night comes on as Earth
   peers like a watery eye through the void
      one bright star glitters low in the west

seven wild geese arrow toward the horizon
   over the streetlights and crouched houses
      the sky deepens from indigo to black

a last faint glimmer of dusk drains away
   cold wind splinters into a thousand stars!
      the roofless sky deepens   night comes on

AT THE BRINK

teetering at the brink of one more spring
a child's heart still thumping in my chest
I'm ready   bring it on!   that first crocus
thrusting up   the first cardinal's bold call
the first rout of glowing daffodils   the first
dogwood blossom bursting open to the sun!

I'm a grass blade who won't stop sprouting
that last glaze of ice melting from the pond
a warm wind kissing the budding branches
a prodigy poking its beak through the shell
I'm turning green and juicy   crafty and wild
I'm scandalous new life irresistibly waking!

teetering at the brink of one more spring
I can't hold back   so I pull out all the stops
these achy old bones start to stumble a jig
what counts is just this reckless urgency
an invincible spirit   my spreading wings
the passion and freedom!   elemental joy!

THE MISTS

the mists   the damps   the darks   lusty lickers!
watch those tiny huge eyes bug out--searchlights
on stalks   not a sunlit blab-alot plausible scene
slippy and squirmy   nightcrawlers sliming a slab

the other edge of nausea--its purging permission
all the fancy freak shops switched off   shut down
here gape shadowy chasms riddled by something
not human   abysses so deep   loving's not known

this whipsawed heart doesn't yearn to resurrect
lost among the never breathing   the never born
how will you croon to entice it back to the living?
what kiss can you pucker tastier than oblivion?

REALITIES

that UFO sighted near an erupting volcano
it's no more ungraspable than each breath
or the bird chirping now outside my window

what am I doing here?   where am I going?
Hubble's wild images explode in my brain!
a million galaxies boogie on the head of a pin!

I'm infinity   whirling at the crux of zero
I'm two plus two equals five   or nothing
I'm a flash in the pan of the cosmic kitchen!

fact is   all bets are off   anything's possible
my sex and age   color and earnings bracket
they can't pigeonhole who I am   who I am

is a riddle wrapped in a mystery
                         sealed by paradox

I could soul kiss you hard twenty-five times
but the twenty-sixth would still be
                         a revelation!

unexplored wormholes blaze inside me
     inconceivable realities burn to be born!

A SMALL WHITE DOG

a small white stray dog I couldn't rescue
was the messenger this time   once more
my heart broke open to love   to the limits
of love   to the bitter edge where love and
the abyss collide in me   and in the world

it sat there   outcast   alone   yet hieratic
dignified   on a plain metal chair in front
of a ramshackle old house   but the renter
would not   could not   feed it or take it in
it sat there with no hope   yet still hoped

what could I do? what if it bit! scratched!
what if it shit in my car on the long drive
to the pound! and even when we got there
what chance did it have? so few get saved
so many are killed   day after deadly day

such are the excuses and evasions I spout
day after deadly day   I long to love vastly
a hero   a saint   a god! but I'm only this
too human hodgepodge of spirit and flesh
part angelic light   part animal selfishness

a small white stray dog I couldn't rescue
was gone the next day when I drove past
fallen through the cracks   lost down that
abyss   or maybe hoping at another door
I bow to my teachers   two-legged or four

CRACKED OPEN

this poem isn't about the looming extinction
of African elephants   now being slaughtered
at a rate even faster than they can reproduce
what can I do?   I've never set foot in Africa

my cringing brain just won't stretch round it
any more than I can save that newborn baby
thrown away in the dumpster   or get there
before the suicide slices deeper into her vein

yet ever since my heart cracked open I can't
not hear   not see   not grasp the enormity
of suffering in the world   I can't block out
stop it   or twitch my horrified self to stone

I try *be here now* and *follow your bliss*
but here and now is each instant everywhere
my soul's bound together with all that's alive
I'm the elephant I kill   I'm this grieving man

THE BALM

a heart is ripped open at sundry places
the morning rain's falling in the cracks

always the rain   the same rain that fell
creating the oceans   watering the first
green thing that grew   primal rain you

don't know grief or loss but like a balm
enter the ravaged crevasses of the heart
cooling   comforting   unknowing   yet
forever salving   serving   always there

rain I raise you as my banner   my cause

you have no face   only a million voices
I'd take hold of your hand if you had one

rain   you don't care if I'm crazy or sane
either way   you promise I'll never thirst

rain   I hear you muttering of my death
chanting my rebirth   soothing   healing

rain   kiss me to sleep in the dark grasses
wake me please to a sweeter wiser world

THE KNOT

I do I don't   I will I won't   mind and heart
two twisted ropes tied into a knot   and not

just any ordinary knot but the mother of all
Gordian Knots   every way I try to solve it

knots it tighter makes it worse   go or stay
take off or kiss   summon my battered self

back to that dangerous arena again   or step
away   turn away   walk away   morph away

I should I shouldn't   I must I couldn't   each
thrust of certainty births its opposite   every

reaching out aborts   recoiling to a pulling in
I'm exhausted thinking about love   blabbing

about love   staggering from love   agonizing
over love! I want out! I need a lovebotomy!

except then I'd taste a loneliness so complete
not all the shoals of stars could comfort me

SPELLBINDER

low   full   and dusky in the east tonight
ancient spellbinder   you compel my eyes
seducing my heart   even though I realize
you're just a barren cratered ball of stone

but that's only one of your many guises
another--intimate companion of my soul
we talk when there's nobody else to listen
what passes between us   I'll never reveal

before oceans filled   mountains thrust up
you were shining   when glaciers first froze
your pallor gleamed across their crevasses
shamans conjured your oracles--entranced!

this night it's just you   me   and the cosmos
beyond loving and loss   death and grieving
I drink deep from your well of what endures
time/eternity   meet in our communion now

I HEARD YOU SAY IT

did you say it? I heard you say it   this joy
we feel now busting out--it's enough! it's all
we need   this sheer joy of being   this grace

did you laugh it? I heard you laughing! yes!
with such irresistible play   your zany voice
drawing forth my own scandalous laughter--

a hilarity zinging from the cosmic Big Bang!
no thoughts   words   or meanings   just bliss
here   now   always   this uncontainable bliss!

did you kiss me? I felt you kiss me   kiss me
like the full moon kissed last night   kiss me
how grass kisses each spring when it sprouts

did you sing the One Name birthing all names
our Secret Name   which only silence knows?
yes   you sang that Name   our Holiest Name!

BLOOD MOON PRAYER

die now   this beating myself over the head
   a persnickety nitpicker   harping away
      at every half-imagined   self-hating fault

be born an incorrigible hugger   embracing
   all brokenhearted dreamers and heroes
      start with the neediest   begin with me

die now   perpetual loser   forever brooding
   on lovers lost   gone   abandoned   rejecting
      harsh words spoken   kind words unsaid

be born dauntless hoper   incurable romantic
   slapstick sucker for a kiss   touch   smile
      still hankering to be ravished by miracle!

die now   too extravagant with a curse   too
   stingy with blessing   old negativity junkie
      wallowing in my hermit's self-pitying sty

be born a fount of gratitude for every instant
   splashing praise   some God-tipsy geyser
      a holy fool cavorting on hilarious feet!

die now   horror of monsters   terror of death
　　swamp-gulper   shadow-muncher   lusting
　　　after obliteration's subversive whore

be born braver   sweeter   wilder   freer
　　life-loving as a child!   be born wondrous
　　　like this harvest moon   shining and serene

TURNING POINT

last week my death snickered from the shadows
even broke into a *tomorrow and tomorrow and
tomorrow* guffaw   my assisted suicide seemed
yummy as a thick slice of fresh warm crumb cake

this week though   just the tiniest pie-in-the-sky
makes my mouth water   bright sun or downpour
dear friend or lost love--I embrace it all   blessed
to be alive and kicking   dumbstruck!   immortal!

what happened that sideswiped my stunned soul
knocking it almost overnight from hell to heaven?
what was the clue   the key   the secret password?
how did this sour grape ripen into a juicy peach?

it's not rocket science   not my conjuring a rabbit
out of a hat   nor any other dazzling magic tricks
not by imagining myself changed   or *the power
of positive thinking*   not through just willing that

on the biting edge of bleak despair I surrendered
not to death   but to One Who forever transcends
I prayed like a monk to unite again with Divinity
joy doesn't come from the world--it starts within!

INVITATION

my death and I met for coffee yesterday
it felt like a first date   we were awkward
shy   hadn't spent time together for ages
I'd so much to tell her! so much to share!

she said she was thinking about me a lot
wanted to go away   wanted me to go too

I was floored   she always confounded me
that rare paradox of reticence and daring
a subtle intimacy   almost too real to bear
her ways of sliding straight into my soul

but abruptly uproot   after so many years?
leave behind friends   job   home   my life?

I told her I needed to pray on it   needed
to mull things over   all the pros and cons
yes I loved her   but did she truly love me?
would she back me through thick and thin?

my heart's bound to yours she answered
I'll hold you tight lover   I'll never let go

QUANDARY

Everything and Nothing   identical twins
except for that freckle on Nothing's cheek

examined up close   it's a pinprick of abyss
a tiny black hole not even love can escape

Everything's the extrovert! full of hijinks
and surprises   a shameless tease and flirt

for Nothing though *still waters run deep*
she watches   waits   a half-smile on her lips

I've dated both and I'm stuck in a quandary
Everything excites! but Nothing's hypnotic

with one I want to laugh   to dance and sing!
with the other   to drown forever in her kiss

Everything and Nothing   each so desirable!
I pendulum between them   unable to decide

SLEEPLESS AFTER A FIGHT

sleepless after a fight with a friend I rise before dawn
   sour acid indigestion   much hurting and remorse
unhappy with him   doubting myself mired yet again
   in the same sick trauma drama   who's right   who's
wrong   why anger erupts   where to go from here

can't see the speck in his eye for the log in my own
   or is it the other way around?   when to stick when
to yield   part of me wants to slam shut the door! but
   another voice says no   wait   try harder   love more
can't tell where his crazies leave off and mine begin

we're dwarfed sometimes by the hugeness of our fear
   greedy to judge   unwilling to forgive   why can't I
live the oneness I preach?   why does he talk the talk
   but not walk the walk?   who fomented such a mess!
all wars start like this--with our fractured humanness

SLAPHAPPY PSALM

You're not here   but everywhere   there's only You
   in the rhythm of my breathing now   the grace of
      silence singing   the dance of my fingers on keys

You're the Secret my scandalous inner child knows
   that Cosmic Joy for which he willingly throws away
      all his glitzy playthings   even mimicries of love

You're my Clown's Face flipped on its ear   laughing!
   My Flash Gordon Decoder Ring   a wild Jump Start
      as my soul's dead battery charges at forty below!

You're the Apple tossed up   but not plunging down
   the Ecstatic Maypole I cavort round like a holy fool
      the Jigsaw Puzzle I'm boggled by   can never solve

You've my Whiplash Windup on the pitcher's mound
   that tasty Sweet Spot where my bat smacks the ball
      the Sting of the line drive just snared in my glove

You're Outrageous Bliss--the Bull's-Eye of the universe!
   the Tickle   the Giggling   the Joke   the Punchline!
      inside outside upside downside   there's only You

CRASH LANDING

I wake up in a bad mood--jittery as a june bug
could a fascist demagogue become president?
that cute housewife from Peoria digs his style
O Lordy! what planet have I crash-landed on?

then the loneliness returns   I start blubbering
my skittish soul lurched off the rails overnight
now I've got a nasty case of the heebie-jeebies
I'm just another refugee   homeless and scared

the crack in the world--it gapes wide inside me
I carry it around like a pet tarantula   feeding it
ragged bits of flesh   spasmodic spurts of blood
who would I be without my voracious sidekick?

desperately   I plead with the Towering Silence
take me back! scour me clean! make me new!
little by little   my alienated self struggles home
to loving again   being loved   on this aching Earth

HERE ON EARTH

time's short and endless here on Earth
moments fly past like buckshot! though
some days drag on and on   as if the sun

stopped   at night that full moon glares
with a hard frozen face   it seems dawn
decides against breaking   skulks away

I'm tiny and immense   snared but free
fearless and terrified   lost   yet found!
mostly   I can't discover which end's up

whole nanoseconds I'm rocked by bliss!
who picked me to make this crazy trip?
why am I stuffed with beans and grace?

then there's you   you're vividly not me
yet you are!   it's me I meet in your yes
or no   frown or kiss   laughter or tears

you're as strange as an albino Martian
familiar as my own rhythmic breathing
we're two pieces of an insoluble jigsaw

it's an unfathomable privilege   isn't it?
this wacky hodgepodge--our being both
human *and* Divine   cosmic music plays

and we lurch around   learning to dance
embrace me lover   I'm raring to boogie
let's grab our chance   let it all hang out!

THE SPLENDOR

sitting alone   not waiting   just being
hearing both outer and inner sounds
at home in the grace of each moment
wanting nothing   nothing's my refuge
peace envelops me   a luminous cloud

sitting alone   outside saturates inside
inside pours out   not divided but One
what do I need to strive for   or prove?
all things flow to me suffused by Light
all things flow from me into the world

sitting alone yet not alone   my solitude
a gateway to the Infinite   I hum a tune
of the happy soul   free offspring of joy!
who's richer than I am right now?   who
lives closer to the Splendor we all seek?

HEARING WIND GUST

hearing wind gust through bare branches
draws me back home to what's elemental
in my bones   their roots still tangled with
the Big Bang   the roil of galaxies forming

an infinitesimally living spark of all this   I
sense I also contain it all   experience it all
all time and space   all dying and becoming
the abyss of the void   the birthing of stars!

when you and I vastly meet   we encounter
as two universes--both familiar and strange
each an uncharted cosmos to the other   yet
each an indispensable portion of the whole

I'm floored by the enormity of a single seed!
stunned by the intimacy of the morning sky!
everything's connected   everything engages
everything's a cryptic companion to my soul

DARKER CRIMSON

a short piece   single cello   with keening violins
it opens my heart's wound so tenderly   achingly

a stroke of darker crimson as the sun slides down
the last longing glance from a dying lover's eyes...

to be a deathless soul   burning in a needy animal
any words   even this music   can only hint at that

all comedy   all tragedy   rocks and rolls around it
a kiss and bite   a laugh and howl   fused into one

if you encounter me here   my strip-searched self
explore with humility   from your own nakedness

then maybe I could bear to be touched   even loved
knowing you shiver to the same bittersweet music

a short piece   single cello   with keening violins
do you feel it?   does it break open your heart too?

THE WOUND

I'm trying to plumb it to the source
the lone spelunker rappelling down
a bottomless abyss   the deeper I go
the farther I sink from air and light

I know it was ripped open by deaths
a sister's cancer   her mother's grief
my father's heart attack   other loves
suffered   lost   abandoned   betrayed

I know a scared child cowers inside it
who runs away and hides   who rages
at heaven   hell   this face-off between
whose trust in love itself was zapped

but it's huger darker colder than these
I plunge back in time beyond one life
to where all creation's agonies tunnel
my taproot drinks from primeval pain

pain that's mine   yours   each being's
Earth's ravaging pain and every star's
pain of any soul spawned by eternity
pain born in the outrageous cry *I AM!*

BIRTH THROES

drawing a blank   it's what always happens
right here at the beginning   without a clue
facing the blind page   anything's possible
what's hardest?   wrestling with emptiness
what's sweetest?   dancing with emptiness
no barriers   no rules or limits   wide open!
such freedom's breathtaking   scary as hell
but I dive in anyway   taking crazy chances

now I flail around in some turbulent ocean
trying not to panic   praying not to drown
the next line pops up like an inflated dingy
and I climb in   hold tight   gasp for breath
roller-coastering these mountainous swells
feels like their coming in eight-line stanzas
if I could just keep afloat for one more line
maybe I can weather this fierce soul-storm

gradually a vast wind subsides   the waves
slacken   here I am again   sitting in a chair
staring at the page   but it's no longer blank
there's a struggle marking it   a raw voyage
as if something naked and primal got born
I'm not sure what that is or why this ruckus
but I want it to live   flourish   grow strong
I want it to exfoliate in me as fearless love!

RIDDLE

if it wasn't so simple   we could solve it
if it wasn't so transparent   we could see

if it wasn't so silent   who'd be listening?
if it wasn't so close   why would we search?

if it wasn't so far   how could we reach it?
if it wasn't so still   when would we dance?

if it wasn't so naked   who'd wear clothes?
if it wasn't so real   why clutch at illusions?

if it wasn't so crazy   how could we stay sane?
if it wasn't so vast   what road would we take?

if it wasn't so absent   when would we meet it?
if it wasn't so empty   where could we rest?

SHOUTING HELLO

something brazenly red is shouting *Hello!*
it's quite far away along the sidewalk as yet
next to a tree and near a parked car   I can't
make out exactly what I'm seeing   just that
it looks huge and round   outrageously red!

drawing closer I realize it's a giant blossom
don't know what kind of flower   but exotic!
with five petals arrayed in a star-like pattern
a chartreuse pistil thrusts out from the center
there's a fragile black stigma flaring at its tip

what amazes me though--the blossom yelled
Hello! hollered from half way down the block
no   not using some humdrum human speech
nor with an articulation my mind could grasp
it sent a scarlet semaphore straight to my soul!

now we stand here   face to face (so to speak)
I feel shy   awkward   don't know what to say
how can I fathom the inner motive of a flower?
but while out walking by myself today I thank
this red blossom for shouting its joyous *Hello!*

OVER THE MOON

to this you've assigned me   O stringent gods
forty years and a day   troubleshooting traffic
at the crossroads of catastrophe and mayhem
my hip flask's sloshing with lukewarm water
all I've got to chew is a wormy crust of bread

shake me   bake me   don't forget to break me
ain't incarnation a hoot?   once upon a crime
I awoke with a clueless grin and this clown's
balloon   now I do pratfalls for chump change
lunging and lurching up the down escalator

wouldn't it be grand to aggravate a geranium
or eat a pile of pickled herring with no hands?
wouldn't I be over the moon--mooning a nun!
no straight laces here   I'll grin and I'll bear it
a narcotic drum bangs   but I'm not marching

who put the trance in Transylvania? who said
we can't remake the rules of this wacky game?
plunging off the pedestal I discover my wings
spreading them wider   I out-horizon the sky!
to this you've inspired me   O merciful gods...

THE ARROW

words miss the Target   the Bull's-Eye
hidden in silence   inaudible   invisible
except to one not listening not looking
just being--both arrow and destination

yet still I write line after line   hoping
to chatter myself nearer the Unsayable
pointing to an absence that's Presence
crying *look! look closer--It's not here!*

why do You forever tease me this way
playing at hide and seek with my soul?
when I search for You I'm left clueless
then I turn--You're miraculously *there!*

anything I say now is also about death
I don't want to die but I feel it waiting
all life long death's been the base beat
a muffled drum throbbing in my bones

soon that time will come when my life
and death embrace in unalloyed ecstasy
at last I'll be free and whole   an arrow
thwacking to rest in the final Bull's-Eye

SOMEBODY NAMED ME

somebody named me said or did that years ago
or just the other day   I cringe now at the memory
was I so chock full of myself? full of something!
I think of words spewed which I can't take back

somebody named me figured the world revolved
around him   prancing stiffly on his high horse
he looked down when he should have looked up
I'm staring into the tarnished mirror of his soul

somebody named me needed a total brain enema
deserved a swift hard kick in the pants   did not
squeeze his too proud feet into another's shoes
I long to ditch him   yet he's my past my shadow

somebody named me was a major league asshole
no doubt he'll relapse--then morph into one again
but now my innermost being's cracked wide open
my Higher Self's awake and penetrates everything!

SOUL'S NEEDLE

I'm sticking with You today Eternal Source
trying to flush out the gringy heebie-jeebies
there's a sick narcissist running for president
and a weird August heatwave in mid-October
bedbugs invading again just down the hall
dead children dragged from bombed houses

hard to get my soul's wobbly needle pivoted
toward eternity I'm caught in heavy traffic
where You squat all week on a median strip
holding up a crudely lettered cardboard sign
while we fidget in our air-conditioned boxes
yearning impatiently for the light to change

I'm zealous and jealous for You Exiled God
You're always the intimate front-page news
yet this radiant bulletin winds up as an obit
the deaf persist in not hearing and the blind
squeeze tightly shut their unperceiving eyes
lonely as hell--to wake among the comatose!

that said I realize on which side my bread's
buttered You're the bread the butter the jam
the juice! You're love's everyday air I breathe
and such sheer stratosphere beyond all breath
whoever doesn't know this now will meet You
on the swells of an Ocean which has no shore...

CARESSES AND WOUNDS

kneeling at my bedroom window   I'm gazing east
after a bleak night of insomnia   at least I'm awake
to watch as luminous tints of pink violet and gold
backlight several trees silhouetted on the horizon

hushed twilight still casts a spell over parked cars
veils patches of grass   shadows the nearby street
a single bird pours out its audacious age-old song
my knees start to hurt   but I just can't turn away

so beauty caresses and wounds at the same time
here now me this dawn   never before or again
I want to hold on forever   yet it's already leaving
as I'm leaving   year after year shedding dead skins

finally I lean on the windowsill   hoist myself up
while the whole sky blooms with brilliant sunrise!
deep inside though   dawn has skewered my soul
this aching won't end until I reach the next world...

AFTER THE ELECTION

at the bookstore the old bearded hippie sitting
behind the counter answered my questions but
he seemed out of it   not stoned but just kind of

far away *I'm in shock* he finally said *I was
sick the day after* and we shook hands on that!
he said he solved what he's been feeling--grief

grief he was right   I felt it too   deep pangs
then numbness   a sharp pain   then numb again
wooziness and disbelief   as if a sister had died

I was another one of the walking wounded   we
were everywhere   when I shopped at Sun Fresh
my friend Jose didn't smile across the vegetables

little by little though   from the core of this ache
something started to blossom   naked and tender
an almost gushing solidarity with total strangers

so when the tiny black lesbian clutching her huge
tank of water got behind me at the checkout line
I stood aside   asked her to please go ahead of me

hate gashes us open   but from this wound a love
pours forth that doesn't calibrate any differences
only says I hurt when you do   and when you heal

then I heal too   hate thinks it has all the answers
but it's already defeated at the moment it strikes
hearts reach out to hearts   there's no end to this...

FAMILY REUNION

faces pressed up against that flimsy pane
the one dividing this world from the next
there you are my beloveds--sister father
mother brother--all floating in the Light

what was splintered into bleeding shards
whole again   who was blinded confused
clear now far-seeing suffused with joy!
I ask your embrace and you give it to me

not with hands or arms   but as Presence
your love no longer contaminated by fear
your eyes   shining conduits of your souls
all my life I've longed and prayed for this

I still sojourn here--a darker colder place
but now you splice my essence to beyond
every breath I draw   I'm breathing you
neither time nor space can keep us apart

A HANDFUL OF CONFETTI

living hell's just about to break loose
an all-American fascist's now elected
president of these divided states with
more raw power to wreck havoc than
any other scary egomaniac in history
meanwhile appalled the numb poet
flings this pathetic handful of confetti
into the abyss what can words save?

when I was born concentration camps
already killed barbarism metastasized
beyond believing grinding up bodies
blasting souls in hatred's meat grinder
how could a child know--the monsters
he feared lurking right under his bed
were real somewhere that very instant
they gobbled a hundred children whole

but that was then over there it ended
we'd won we beat them! it couldn't
happen *again* it couldn't happen *here*
not in the Land of the Free the Home
of the Brave! didn't we witness horror?
depravity? inhumanity so shameful it
splintered the mind ravaged the heart?
didn't we defeat the monster *inside us?*

apparently not   or at least not enough
I've lived too long   I've lived to hear
neighbors cheer a bully   a demagogue
who stirs and stokes the worst in them
I've lived to hear self-righteous patriots
parrot the vilest garbage as their gospel
I've lived to hear fervent "Christians"
pound the drums for scapegoat blood

yet still I fling this handful of confetti
into the abyss   I was born a dreamer
and I guess I'll die as one   my heart
breaks for my country   for our world
for those many who soon must suffer
far more than a grieving old poet may
when will we stop our insanity? when
will we learn to live in universal love...

DETACHMENT

detachment's what I most need right now
but it's what I appear least able to muster
awake half the night obsessed about...well
anything everything nothing whatever

my death will detach me quite completely
and I ought to rehearse for that *"shuffling
off this mortal coil"* but instead I'm stuck
in my anxious needy hopeful hopeless self
a creature cuffed around by my own fears

I study the teachings of the wise masters
try every way I know to humbly live them
yet here I am regardless   still mired in me
have I been racing up the down escalator?
shadow-boxing with my mirrored image?
I'm stumbling one step forward--two back

how splendid it would be--to ditch my ego!
I mean really truly totally empty me out
till nobody's left but a vessel for divine joy!
but how terrifying--stripped of my ballast!
worry beads are my catechism   my rosary

at least I see what cries to be done--let go!
let go of the delusion I could be in control
let go of the farce I know which end is up
let go even of this demand I need to let go

AS ABOVE SO BELOW

branch or root   bloom or seed
sun or moon   blue sky or rain
summer or winter   mind or gut
daytime or night   fire or water
yes or *no*   the truth be told
as above so below   all are One

strive or cease   talk or silence
history or myth   hero or clown
south or north   teach or learn
cloud or cave   logic or dream
rights or laws   the truth be told
as above so below   all are One

rising or sinking   fly or crawl
fame or failure   star or stone
rich or poor   laughter or tears
full or empty   fertile or barren
life or death   the truth be told
as above so below   all are One

GRAINS OF SILENCE

how a stone waits   be that again   hold
grains of silence secreted through ages

it never blabs   doesn't demand anything
won't trouble your heart with opinions

yet inside it--millenniums! Himalayas
of change   eons of worlds compressed

be patient like a stone   try not to fidget
get over making huge pronouncements

there's a dark that sheds light   a peace
which summons you to oceanic depths

here's the source   your beginning place
before life   after death   beyond thought

you built fabulous sandcastles of words
now the tide rolls in   washes them away

DESERT NIGHTS

there's sitting all alone in a swivel chair
there's standing and walking somewhere
there's snarfing that same cheap granola
there's insomnia   and yearning for dawn
there's the round world again shrunk flat

this list could go on forever   *"tomorrow
and tomorrow"* I strain to squeeze blood
from a stone   thirst for rain in the desert
my brain scuttles like a famished scorpion
wherever I go here I am   cornered in me

I stare into the abyss   it stares right back
I slap my face to make sure I'm still alive
the full moon must be outside somewhere
hanging with those pinpricks called stars
not trails I can follow   no pathway there

keeping it real's a bitch when you can't
even find your own sorry ass in the dark
enlightenment shrivels down to survival
revelation?　take one breath then another
praying that once more   the sun will rise

DIVINE STALKING
(for Deepak Chopra)

the other day I glanced in the mirror and there
God was a little worse for wear staring back
through bloodshot eyes so I watched myself
watching myself tightrope-walking the dawn

then later on you flashed your contagious grin
and God was smiling at me with such zaniness
seems like I can't shake off this Divine stalking
look! here's the redbud tree blossoming glory!

what if we inherit a different kind of breathing
a deep suspiration of the spirit that sustains us
every boggling instant! what if we're on Earth
to wake up--finally reclaim our boundlessness!

I don't want to sound too simplistic about this
every awful instant a baby starves somewhere
we slaughter each other--deranged carnivores
oblivious to the trampled sanctity of our souls

yet my eyes your smile the redbud blooming
keep urging another story a way we can grow
from half lost part hollow living dead things
into knowing that we and the universe are one

NORTH WIND

north wind   rattling the panes   be my teacher
so my voice might grow as elemental as yours
strip it clean of everything that's not bone-real
scour my ego away until silence wears speech
its tumultuous veil rippling spells and oracles

unless these words are set to such stark music
they're foolish paltry tricks   mere Tinker-Toys
I fumble about with   compel me to listen close
lost to myself   hidden deep inside the weather
keening the high cold wild free truth you chant

north wind   you've been breathing me forever
before I was born you sieved through my soul
on the first day I left home   in that schoolyard
I stood stunned as a fierce gust swooped down
without knowing   yet I *knew*   all was changed

if I could tell a single shred of that knowledge!
if I could translate one syllable you sang to me!
if the north wind itself rushed from my throat
riddled with bird cries   with cosmic distances!
maybe then I could say I conceived a true poem

MESSENGER

leaning against a shelf in the supermarket's
produce department   I'm concentrating on
the weekly food ad sales   neither happy nor
sad   just going about my everyday business

when glancing over the top of a page   I see
a tiny dark-haired Hispanic girl--about five
shyly holding up an ad section I've dropped
she beams at me with spontaneous gladness

my breath stops   for a split second I'm fazed
dumbfounded   staring into the face of...Who?
there are no words   simply her radiant bliss
offering me a handful of unconditional love

there are no words yet I'm groping for words
what's left to say?   The Source of All-That-Is
embraced me through a child's countenance!
my naked soul melts   tears brim at my eyes

messengers address us each hour of existence
and the revelations always pare down to this:
*Wake Up! open your heart! break the chains
that keep you from living your own Divinity!*

EXCERPTS FROM
THE DEMON TACTICS GUIDE

It always dangles your worst addictions as bait
It licks raw wounds down to their exposed nerve
It smirks and strokes   fondles your naked vanity
It lurks at your blind side   lusts for the ambush
It knows no shame as it lewdly croons your guilt
It lathers on the disguise of your contrariest love
It preens when you feel like shower curtain scum
It savors your despair as some exquisite aperitif
It seduces you to betray your innermost ecstasy
It crazy-makes you with forever switched signals
It smugly accuses you of Its own transgressions
It glares back rudely through a fun house mirror
It infests the shadow you've amputated from soul

THE LIMITS
(for John)

came then to the limits of love
but never realized it   thinking
if I was grown up   I'd save her
rescue her   but eight years old
I was already plunged into acid
already scathed from too much
knowing of too much pain so I
ran away inside fiercely played
blocked out the thing on the bed
the skull and crossed bones that
once was my sister once was my
playmate and friend   yet the rest
of my life I sought to conjure her
back from the grave the hurt boy
still raging still refusing to accept
how it is--the sweet *and* the bitter

we're born to cherish what suffers
and dies   born to break our hearts
on the rocks of grief   born to learn
too soon too late the limits of love

INVOKING THE MUSE

all cracked and banged up though I be
consecrate me as Your vessel in service
to The Most High   flood my hollowness
let it brim over with clangorous speech
waking sleepwalkers from their trance
stopping the ball busters in their tracks

all battered and tarnished though it be
upraise this voice--revelation's trumpet
lifting the broken heart   the fearful soul
praising the Divine Source of all-that-is
scour it clean then polish it to gleaming
I soar my glad hallelujah for God alone!

all damaged and incomplete as we are
ever teach and guide us Invisible Ones
inspire us to levitate beyond our griefs
tasting undreamt wavelengths of light
fixing our wide-open eyes on eternity!
help us see--we've always been Home

SHINING ONES

it's hard--not to hear You or see You
yet still believe You're there--Guides
from a Higher World   Shining Ones

the part of me that's a dying animal
runs scared at every stress and pain
each night I do the insomnia shuffle

and what about our frantic so-called
"civilization"? terror hell and death
erupt! it's as American as apple pie

we took a wrong turn centuries ago
abandoning wise Invisible Teachers
worshiping the human mind instead

where once we discovered our souls
now we stare into the howling void
and shudder with cosmic loneliness

nevertheless I rise   report for duty
crouching at these bleak front lines
facing the emptiness keening inside

dropping to sore and bloodied knees
chanting out my love   still believing
You're there for us   O Shining Ones

METAMORPHOSIS

the large butterfly is dazzling yellow
with black streaks on its wings and
a black fringe around the edges   it

sips nectar from those tiny clustered
violet blossoms   flitting to one then
another   I stand watching entranced

we never know what we'll encounter
just stepping out our door every day--
a clown holding a polka-dot balloon

the raw stump of a chainsawed tree
a long-lost lover   now reincarnated
as some rare yellow-black butterfly

our choice is simple but stark   hide
encased in the ego's glittering armor
or strip down radically to naked soul

wide open to each unknown we meet
trusting that only thus we'll discover
who we are and why we sojourn here

the large butterfly is dazzling yellow
with black streaks on my wings and
a black fringe around the edges   I

savor nectar from the tiny clustered
violet blossoms   flitting to one then
another   gladly gone into the Glory

I was born and raised in New York City, attending the public schools there—a pretty typical kid, gabby and obnoxious, who loved to play with his friends. But when I was eight years old, my four-year-old sister Carole Anne was diagnosed with liver cancer. We watched her wither away to a living skeleton, then die in agony. The soul of our family was shattered. The poetry I began writing as an adolescent seeped from that grieving wound, expressed that stark alienation. And that's where my essential self remained until, as a 32-year old atheist, my soul was suddenly cracked open. I experienced an overwhelming mystical awakening which forever changed my life.

Well before this great turning point, I'd graduated from Queens College, N. Y., earning a B.A. In Creative Writing while winning a couple of literary awards: The Dwight V. Durling Poetry Prize, and The Peter Pauper Press Award. I was also very active in college theater, playing several leading roles. Prior to graduating however, I dropped out for a while, studied acting at HB Studios in Greenwich Village, then served in the U.S. Army Military Police, gaining an honorable discharge. Eventually, I moved to Kansas City, Mo., completing most classes toward a Masters in English Lit. at UMKC, but not taking a degree. Except for three years in the St. Louis area, I've lived in Kansas City ever since.

The many jobs I've held to support my *vision quest* have included hotel package clerk and porter, social service worker, newspaper reporter, education writer, mental health technician, house painter, chemical plant worker, lumberyard pallet maker, exterminator, program instructor for the developmentally disabled, group home supervisor, shipping clerk, silk screener, paste-up artist, warehouse worker, health equipment tester, bookseller, and security guard.

On the creative side, I was a co-founder of K.C.'s original Prospero's Pit Open Mic; taught a *Poetry Of Spirit* class through Communiversity for many years, and currently I'm a member of K.C.'s Mystic Poets Society.

I've published five books of poetry: *Report From The Frontier: Selected Poems,* UD Press, 2003; *Black Butterfly: Poems For A Muse,* Dog Ear Publications, 2009; *Cosmic Consciousness: Songs of an Ecstatic Soul,* International Publishers, 2016; and the two chapbooks—*Manifesto For The Muse,* 1999, and *Shape Shifter,* 2005, both from Wing-And-A-Prayer Press.

This project was made possible, in part, by generous support from the Osage Arts Community.

Osage Arts Community provides temporary time, space and support for the creation of new artistic works in a retreat format, serving creative people of all kinds — visual artists, composers, poets, fiction and nonfiction writers. Located on a 152-acre farm in an isolated rural mountainside setting in Central Missouri and bordered by ¾ of a mile of the Gasconade River, OAC provides residencies to those working alone, as well as welcoming collaborative teams, offering living space and workspace in a country environment to emerging and mid-career artists. For more information, visit us at www.oac.com

Osage Arts Community

www.ingramcontent.com/pod-product-compliance
Lightning Source LLC
Chambersburg PA
CBHW021450080526
44588CB00009B/777